THE CENTER FOR PREVENTIVE ACTION

Afghanistan's Uncertain Transition From Turmoil to Normalcy

Barnett R. Rubin

CSR NO. 12, MARCH 2006
COUNCIL ON FOREIGN RELATIONS

Founded in 1921, the Council on Foreign Relations is an independent, national membership organization and a nonpartisan center for scholars dedicated to producing and disseminating ideas so that individual and corporate members, as well as policymakers, journalists, students, and interested citizens in the United States and other countries, can better understand the world and the foreign policy choices facing the United States and other governments. The Council does this by convening meetings; conducting a wide-ranging Studies program; publishing *Foreign Affairs*, the preeminent journal covering international affairs and U.S. foreign policy; maintaining a diverse membership; sponsoring Independent Task Forces and Special Reports; and providing up-to-date information about the world and U.S. foreign policy on the Council's website, www.cfr.org.

THE COUNCIL TAKES NO INSTITUTIONAL POSITION ON POLICY ISSUES AND HAS NO AFFILIATION WITH THE U.S. GOVERNMENT. ALL STATEMENTS OF FACT AND EXPRESSIONS OF OPINION CONTAINED IN ITS PUBLICATIONS ARE THE SOLE RESPONSIBILITY OF THE AUTHOR OR AUTHORS.

Council Special Reports (CSRs) are concise policy briefs, produced to provide a rapid response to a developing crisis or contribute to the public's understanding of current policy dilemmas. CSRs are written by individual authors—who may be Council fellows or acknowledged experts from outside the institution—in consultation with an advisory committee, and typically take sixty days or less from inception to publication. The committee serves as a sounding board and provides feedback on a draft report. It usually meets twice—once before a draft is written and once again when there is a draft for review; however, advisory committee members, unlike Task Force members, are not asked to sign off on the report or to otherwise endorse it. Once published, CSRs are posted on the Council's website.

For further information about the Council or this Special Report, please write to the Council on Foreign Relations, 58 East 68th Street, New York, NY 10021, or call the Communications office at 212-434-9400. Visit our website at www.cfr.org.

CONTENTS

FOREWORD

Stabilization and reconstruction operations in Afghanistan have been overshadowed by developments in Iraq since the 2003 invasion. This overshadowing detracts from the achievements in Afghanistan since 2001, including the completion of the benchmarks in the Bonn Agreement, which has given Afghanistan a constitutional framework and nascent political institutions. However, much hard work remains before these institutions can be considered mature. Moreover, the security situation has deteriorated significantly, and long-term stability in Afghanistan remains elusive.

The January 2006 Afghanistan Compact rightly reminds international actors to be mindful that Afghanistan's transition to what might be described as normalcy is not yet assured and that strong international engagement will be essential to address remaining challenges. This report, supported by a generous grant from the Carnegie Corporation of New York, analyzes the challenges Afghanistan faces, including sensitive issues not addressed in the compact, and proposes measures to meet them. By delineating tasks in the areas of security, governance, reconstruction, and regional cooperation that still require significant attention and resources, this report makes an important contribution to our understanding of what should be done in a country whose importance has for too long and too often been underestimated.

Richard N. Haass
President
Council on Foreign Relations
March 2006

ACKNOWLEDGMENTS

I would like to thank William L. Nash, director of the Center for Preventive Action at the Council on Foreign Relations, for initiating and overseeing this project, Richard N. Haass and James M. Lindsay of the Council for their support, and the Carnegie Corporation of New York for their generous grant that supported this work. I benefited a great deal from comments received by teleconference and email by the advisory group for this report, most especially Joseph J. Collins, Laura K. Cooper, James F. Dobbins, Bathsheba N. Crocker, S. Frederick Starr, Reuben E. Brigety II, Jonathan E. Berman, Pamela Constable, and Peter Warren Singer.

I also received extensive and detailed comments from senior officials at the U.S. embassy and Coalition headquarters in Kabul. Clare Lockhart of the Overseas Development Institute provided helpful perspective. Peter Middlebrook, Mohammad Eshaq, Husain Haqqani, Saad Mohseni, and a senior Afghan official provided invaluable comments. I benefited greatly from reports on the research of Idrees Rahmani, an international policy fellow of the Open Society Institute. Abubaker Saddique, Humayun Hamidzada, and Abby Stoddard of the Center on International Cooperation provided comments and research assistance.

Jamie Ekern of the Center for Preventive Action shepherded numerous drafts every step of the way, arranged meetings among people (especially me) in far-flung locations, and tracked down references.

If all of these people and institutions had agreed with what I had written, their advice would not have been nearly so valuable. I am sure that many will disagree, and neither they nor the Council on Foreign Relations, bear any responsibility for the views expressed herein, which are solely mine.

Barnett R. Rubin

MAPS

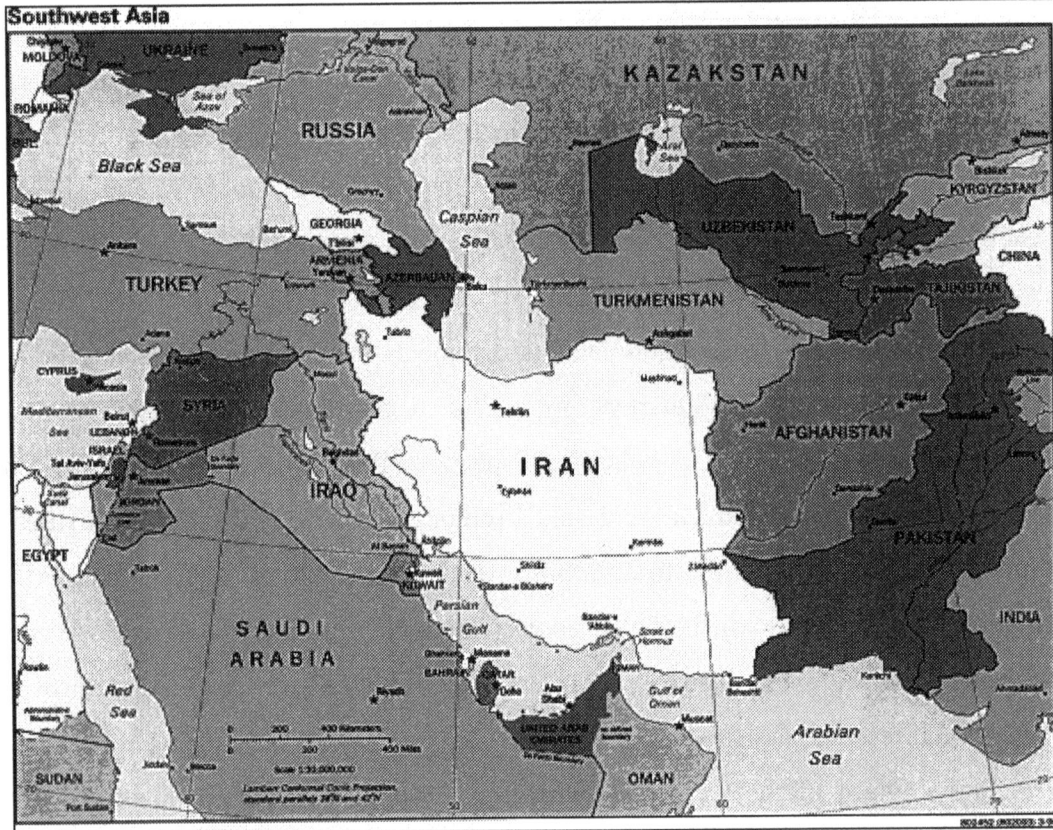

Map 1: Southwest Asia

Source: Map graphic provided by maps.com.

Map 2: Afghanistan

ACRONYMS

ANA	Afghan National Army
ANP	Afghan National Police
ANDS	Afghanistan National Development Strategy
CDC	Community Development Council
DIA	Defense Intelligence Agency
DIAG	disbandment of illegal armed groups
G8	Group of Eight
GDP	gross domestic product
I-ANDS	Interim Afghanistan National Development Strategy
IMF	International Monetary Fund
ISAF	International Security Assistance Force
NATO	North Atlantic Treaty Organization
NSP	National Solidarity Program
PRT	Provincial Reconstruction Team
SSR	security sector reform
UNDP	United Nations Development Programme

INTRODUCTION:

THE AFGHANISTAN COMPACT

Before the terrorist attacks of September 11, 2001, and all that followed, Afghans and the handful of internationals working on Afghanistan could hardly have imagined being fortunate enough to confront today's problems. The Bonn Agreement of December 2001 providing for the "reestablishment of permanent government institutions" in Afghanistan was fully completed with the adoption of a constitution in January 2004, the election of President Hamid Karzai in October 2004, and the formation of the National Assembly in December 2005.

From January 31 to February 1, 2006, President Karzai, UN Secretary-General Kofi Annan, and British Prime Minister Tony Blair presided over a conference in London of about sixty states and international organizations that issued the Afghanistan Compact, setting forth both the international community's commitment to Afghanistan and Afghanistan's commitment to state-building and reform over the next five years. The compact supports the Afghan National Development Strategy (ANDS), an interim version of which (I-ANDS) the Afghan government presented at the conference.[1] The compact provides a strategy for building an effective, accountable state in Afghanistan, with targets for improvements in security, governance, and development, including measures for reducing the narcotics economy and promoting regional cooperation.[2] The compact also prescribes ways for the Afghan government and donors to make aid more effective and establishes a mechanism to monitor adherence to the timelines and benchmarks. The compact places responsibility for meeting these goals on the government of Afghanistan, which can easily be held accountable, and the "international community," which cannot be. The United States, United Kingdom, and other donors strongly opposed language in the compact that would have held those present at the London conference (listed in a compact annex), rather than an abstract entity, responsible for implementation.

---

[1] The Afghanistan Compact and the I-ANDS are available at www.ands.gov.af.
[2] For this conceptual framework for peace building, see Barnett R. Rubin, "Constructing Sovereignty for Security," *Survival*, Vol. 47, No. 4 (Winter 2005), pp. 93–106.

During his visit to Afghanistan, India, and Pakistan from March 1 to March 5, 2006, President George W. Bush praised Afghan successes, telling President Karzai, "You are inspiring others, and the inspiration will cause others to demand their freedom." He did so the day after the administration's own intelligence chiefs reported that the antigovernment insurgency in Afghanistan is growing and presents a greater threat "than at any point since late 2001."[3] Some Afghan officials say the world thus far has put Afghanistan on life support, rather than investing in a cure. The following conditions make it clear that Afghanistan has the potential to be a disasterous situation if intelligent, measured steps are not taken:

- An ever-more deadly insurgency with sanctuaries in neighboring Pakistan, where leaders of al-Qaeda and the Taliban have found refuge;
- A corrupt and ineffective administration without resources and a potentially dysfunctional parliament;
- Levels of poverty, hunger, ill health, illiteracy, and gender inequality that put Afghanistan near the bottom of every global ranking;
- Levels of aid that have only recently expanded above a fraction of that accorded to other post-conflict countries;
- An economy and administration heavily influenced by drug traffickers;
- Massive arms stocks despite the demobilization of many militias;
- A potential denial of the Islamic legitimacy of the Afghan government by a clergy that feels marginalized;
- Ethnic tensions exacerbated by competition for resources and power;
- Interference by neighboring states, all of which oppose a long-term U.S. presence in the region;
- Well-trained and well-equipped security forces that the government may not be able to pay when aid declines in a few years;
- Constitutional requirements to hold more national elections (at least six per decade) than the government may be able to afford or conduct;

---

[3] Walter Pincus, "Growing Threat Seen In Afghan Insurgency: Defense Intelligence Agency Chief Cites Surging Violence in Homeland," *Washington Post*, March 1, 2006.

- An exchange rate inflated by aid and drug money that subsidizes cheap imports and hinders economic growth; and
- Future generations of unemployed, frustrated graduates and dropouts from the rapidly expanding school system.

The compact addresses these challenges insofar as is possible in an international declaration. Its principal recommendation is that all stakeholders should fully fund and implement the Afghanistan Compact and the I-ANDS. This Council Special Report makes some additional recommendations, organized according to the three pillars of the compact and I-ANDS: security; governance, rule of law, and human rights; and economic and social development. As in those documents, counternarcotics and regional cooperation are treated as crosscutting issues.

Recommendations elaborate on the following themes:

- Afghanistan has received inadequate resources in terms of both troops and funds; this is not the time to draw down the military presence or to reduce aid.
- Afghanistan can be stable and secure only if it is well integrated into its region, both economically and politically. Achieving this goal will require sustained efforts to deescalate and eventually resolve the country's long-standing conflicts with Pakistan over relations with India, the border, ethnic issues, and transit trade, and to insulate Afghanistan from conflict relating to Iran.
- None of the problems of this destitute, devastated country can be addressed effectively without sustained, equitable economic growth. In addition to security, this requires extensive investments in infrastructure, governance, and the justice system.
- Economic growth also requires a policy of eliminating narcotics that does not impoverish people. There should be no short-term conditionality of aid on eliminating narcotics. Elimination of narcotics will take well over a decade, and crop eradication is a counterproductive way to start such a program. Foreign donors should support the Afghan government's long-term plan and not impose their own programs.
- A stable and secure Afghanistan requires a legitimate and capable state. To ensure that international aid fulfills this objective, the United States and other major aid

donors that have not done so already, notably Germany and Japan, should provide multiyear aid commitments and channel increasing amounts of aid through the government budget by mechanisms such as the Afghanistan Reconstruction Trust Fund, the Law and Order Trust Fund for Afghanistan, and the Counter-Narcotics Trust Fund for Afghanistan.

SECURITY

There are two international military commands in Afghanistan: the U.S.-led Coalition and the International Security Assistance Force (ISAF). The Coalition, whose primary mission is defined as counterterrorism and counterinsurgency, and which enjoys freedom of action under the United States' right of self defense, came to Afghanistan to assure first the security of Americans from al-Qaeda and then of the Afghan government from the insurgency.[4] ISAF's mission is to help the Afghan authorities provide security according to the Bonn Agreement, relevant UN Security Council resolutions, and a bilateral agreement with the Afghan government.

The avowed goal of both commands is to provide security directly until Afghan security forces are prepared to do so themselves. Building Afghan national capacity to provide security requires the policies known as security sector reform (SSR), including both the dissolution of irregular armed groups through demobilization, disarmament, and reintegration, and the creation or transformation of previous forces into professional units.

Both the Coalition and ISAF have operated with a light footprint that has been inadequate to deliver security.[5] Achieving this goal has also been hampered by lack of coordination between the two commands' different definitions of security priorities. The Coalition armed and funded Afghan commanders to seize and hold ground after the Taliban and al-Qaeda fled the U.S. air offensive. Some of these commanders used the money and arms they received to invest in drug production and engage in land grabs, predation, political intimidation, and ethnic cleansing—a major source of insecurity for Afghans. Meanwhile, ISAF first deployed to Kabul, and then elsewhere, to provide

---

[4] The United States began building a "coalition of the willing" against terrorism on September 12, 2001; there are currently seventy nations supporting the global war on terrorism. To date, twenty-one nations have deployed more than 16,000 troops to the U.S. Central Command's region of responsibility. In Afghanistan, Coalition partners are contributing approximately 8,000 troops to Operation Enduring Freedom and to the ISAF in Kabul. See http://www.centcom.mil/sites/uscentcom1/Shared%20Documents/Coalition.aspx.

[5] Michael Bhatia et al., "Minimal Investments, Minimal Results: The Failure of Security Policy in Afghanistan," Afghanistan Research and Evaluation Unit, June 2004; James Dobbins et al., *America's Role in Nation-Building: From Germany to Iraq* (Santa Monica: RAND, 2003); Seth G. Jones, "Averting Failure in Afghanistan," *Survival*, Vol. 48, No. 1 (Spring 2006).

security from the commanders allied with the Coalition, as well as from Taliban and al-Qaeda. The militias allied with the Coalition were supposed to withdraw from areas occupied by ISAF; they did not, and the United States declined to press them to do so. Although ISAF has helped prevent factional clashes in Kabul, the militias' continued presence in Kabul, regional cities, and border posts provided them with political leverage and the ability to engage in predation and trafficking.

By mid-2002, U.S. commanders on the ground understood the need to provide Afghans with reconstruction and governance to consolidate military gains, despite the administration's original opposition to "nation-building" and "peacekeeping." Although the Pentagon continued to oppose ISAF expansion until late 2003 (and other countries were not exactly lining up to volunteer), ground commanders won approval for Coalition-led Provincial Reconstruction Teams (PRTs). PRTs are small, joint civilian-military organizations. These deployments of dozens of people—predominantly from the military, with a few embedded civilian aid providers—are intended to create an "ISAF effect without ISAF." In the summer and fall of 2003, when the Pentagon relaxed its opposition, the North Atlantic Treaty Organization (NATO) took command of ISAF and started extending it outside of Kabul. Germany, Spain, Canada, and other NATO members, who wanted to find a way to affirm their alliance with the United States, despite opposition to the invasion of Iraq, now stepped forward to contribute, although sometimes with restrictive national caveats on their operations. NATO took on PRTs as the template for expansion. NATO and the Coalition have since worked out a plan for nationwide coverage by PRTs in four stages. The United States, whose forces are overextended due to the war in Iraq, would like to withdraw forces as ISAF expansion continues, leading to the unification of command with a common mission. Because the U.S. Coalition has presided over a strengthening rather than defeat of the insurgency, however, NATO troops would have to engage in active combat, which most alliance members are not prepared to do.

The compact calls on both the Coalition and ISAF to continue support of the Afghan government's efforts to establish security and stability, including commitments to carry out "counterterrorism" operations in close coordination with the government, expand coverage by PRTs, help disband illegal armed groups, and build fiscally sustainable military and police forces bound by the rule of law.

INSURGENCY

After years of claiming that greater American and Afghan casualties are either signs of "desperation" by foundering terrorists or the result of more aggressive U.S. tactics that are pushing opposition fighters out of their safe havens, the U.S. government has now admitted that the insurgency is growing and becoming more effective. U.S. and Afghan government casualties caused by the insurgency are higher in 2005 than in any previous year (see figure 1). Insurgent activities have increased in lethality, with increased use of tactics seen in Iraq, including suicide bombings, which the Defense Intelligence Agency (DIA) estimates have quadrupled in the past year, and improvised explosive devises, whose use has doubled. According to Ahmed Rashid, a Pakistani journalist based in Lahore, "In the past few months, at least thirty attacks have killed nearly one hundred people in Afghanistan, including NATO peacekeepers and a Canadian diplomat."[6] Afghanistan and the Arab world have now switched places: whereas before 9/11 Arab jihadists created a base for terrorism in Afghanistan, the war in Iraq now provides a training and testing ground for new jihadi tactics, which have spread to Afghanistan.

The Coalition and the Afghan government have disagreed over the diagnosis of the insurgency and the strategy against it. The United States is largely relying on cooperation with Pakistan for action against al-Qaeda and Taliban sanctuaries in that country, although President Bush has noted that more needs to be done.[7] The Coalition is also waging aggressive campaigns against insurgency sanctuaries in Afghanistan and trying to increase development and governance efforts in areas of Taliban activity through PRTs and civil affairs projects. Although during his March 2006 visit President Bush praised both President Karzai and President Pervez Musharraf as staunch allies in the war on terror, the two presidents were waging an active war of words against each

---

[6] Ahmed Rashid, "He's Welcome in Pakistan," *Washington Post*, February 26, 2006.
[7] "Bush Praises Pakistan Terror Role," BBC News, March 4, 2006.

other in the media both before and after his visit. Relations deteriorated rapidly, with little apparent action by the United States to address this conflict.

Figure 1: Growth in Insurgency: Attacks on and Fatalities of Coalition and Government Forces in Afghanistan, 2002–2005

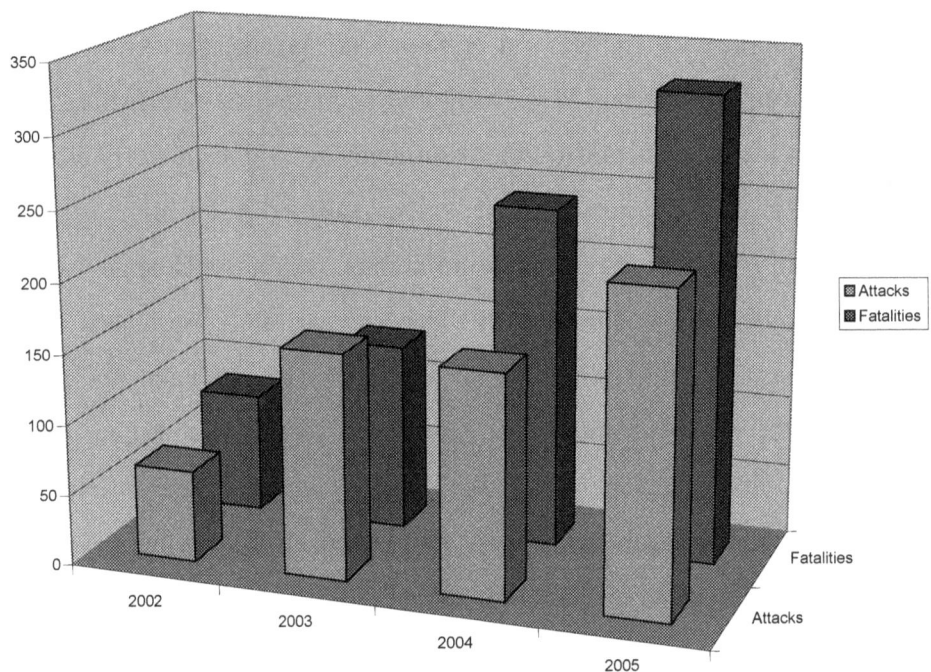

Source: Data from RAND-MIPT Terrorism Incident Database, courtesy of Seth Jones.

The Afghan government wants Washington to reduce unpopular actions inside Afghanistan, reduce its unilateral actions, and instead focus pressure on Pakistan. Karzai has stated that, "No coalition forces should go to Afghan homes without the authorization of the Afghan government....The use of air power is something that may not be very effective now."[8]

---

[8] Daniel Cooney, "Karzai Wants End to U.S.-Led Operations," *Associated Press Online* (Kabul), September 20, 2005.

8

Yet more than four years after the initial offensive and the establishment of what is supposed to be a fully sovereign Afghan government, U.S. forces and their contractors still enjoy full "freedom of action" without any status of forces agreement. The Bush administration's insistence on independence for U.S. forces and impunity for contractors is undermining support for Coalition presence, damaging its sustainability.

The government of Afghanistan also has discreetly joined the global chorus of protest over the mistreatment of detainees by the Bush administration. During his Washington visit in May 2005, President Karzai asked for the transfer of Afghan detainees to his government's custody and for more control by Afghanistan over Coalition operations. The United States has since signed an agreement for the gradual transfer of Afghan detainees, although the Afghan government protested the failure to adequately punish U.S. soldiers for the torture and murder of two detainees in Bagram air base and the sacrilegious burning of the bodies of Taliban who had died in battle.[9]

The Joint Declaration of Strategic Partnership of May 17, 2005, providing for "freedom of action" by U.S. forces must give way to a status of forces agreement between Afghanistan and the United States that affirms Afghan sovereignty, commits both sides to respect international humanitarian law, and limits threats to neighboring states from U.S. bases.[10] Such an agreement should regulate the legal status of detainees and U.S. contractors on the basis of international law. It also should make clear that the U.S. presence in Afghanistan is directed solely at combating terrorism and insurgency and that Afghanistan will not become a permanent U.S. base.

Such an agreement alone, however, would not constitute a counterinsurgency strategy. The strategy also has to emphasize an end to foreign sanctuaries and the strengthening of the Afghan government and economy in affected areas. More aggressive military action by the Coalition in the past year has led to successful adaptation by the insurgents. The Pentagon's plan to reduce U.S. coalition forces from 20,000 to 16,000 represents only a return to the levels of 2004 and is supposed to be compensated for by deployment of British, Canadian, and Dutch forces to southern Afghanistan, but it is causing anxiety in Kabul as a sign of decreasing U.S. commitment. This anxiety may not

---

[9] Tim Golden, "Years After Two Afghans Died, Case Falters," *New York Times*, February 13, 2006.
[10] The White House, *Press Release: Joint Declaration of the United States-Afghanistan Strategic Partnership*, May 23, 2005. See http://www.state.gov/p/sa/rls/pr/2005/46628.htm.

be justified on military grounds. The UK and Canada, in particular, have extensive experience in ISAF. The chief of staff of the Canadian armed forces, General Rick J. Hillier, is a former ISAF commander who is well regarded for his innovations and strategic thinking. These units, experienced in peace support and counterinsurgency activities, may be at least as effective as the U.S. forces, despite the latter's superior firepower. Nonetheless, the decision by the United States to reduce forces at the same time that its intelligence agencies have reached a consensus that the insurgent threat is greater than ever has sent the wrong message about U.S. commitment. Reversal of this relatively small reduction would reassure Afghans and send a clear message to the entire region.

STRATEGY TOWARD PAKISTAN AND THE REST OF THE REGION

Studies of insurgency indicate that logistical and support networks are critical to their survival. The U.S. and Afghan governments agree that, despite Pakistan's denial, the Taliban enjoy "safe havens" there, but they differ in their analysis of the role of official policy.[11] Success is not possible without a coherent U.S. strategy not only toward Pakistan and Afghanistan but also toward the Pakistan-Afghanistan relationship. This relationship, which has been tense for most of the last sixty years, has been the source of much of the region's instability and is today the key factor assuring continued sanctuary for the Taliban, foreign jihadists, and other extremists. The current antagonistic relations between the two countries mimic previous relations between the two states during most of the period since 1947, when Pakistan gained independence in its current borders over the objections of Afghanistan, which challenged the incorporation of the Pashtun areas. The Bush administration has treated both governments as allies in the "War on Terror" and has seemed tone-deaf to the historically troubled relations between them, which continue to pose obstacles to the cooperation needed for success. The March 2006

---

[11] For a critical view from a former Pakistani insider, see Husain Haqqani, "Pakistan is Playing a Cat and Mouse Game," *Gulf News*, October 19, 2005, http://www.gulf-news.com/Articles/WorldNF.asp?Article ID=187493. Also see Haqqani's book, *Pakistan: Between Mosque and Military* (Washington, DC: Carnegie Endowment for International Peace, 2005).

presidential visit to the region, which also featured unprecedented concessions to India on the development of nuclear power that underscored Pakistan's insecurity, exacerbated the antagonism between Kabul and Islamabad.

Many Afghans, apparently including President Karzai, believe that the Taliban could not operate from Pakistan without official support. President Karzai has urged the Coalition to "concentrate on where terrorists are trained, on their bases, on the supply to them, [and] on the money coming to them."[12] Many members of the current Afghan government, including the president and minister of defense, worked for mujahidin groups in Pakistan during the 1980s and are intimately familiar with Pakistan's intelligence agencies and covert action structure. President Karzai also has revived the relations between the Afghan state and Pashtun tribal and political leaders in Pakistan. He met some of them, including outspoken opponents of President Musharraf, during his February 15–16 visit to Pakistan. In this Afghan view, the continued insurgency signals that stability in Afghanistan cannot be achieved at the expense of Pakistan's interests, particularly regarding an Indian presence in Afghanistan. Afghanistan has never recognized the British-drawn Durand Line dividing the Pashtun areas as an international border; the cross-border insurgency pressures Afghanistan to accept the border as the price for stabilizing it. Additionally, Pakistan may wish to keep its options open against the day that the United States withdraws.

President Musharraf, however, characterized Karzai's charges that Pakistan is harboring Taliban leaders, terrorists, and suicide bombers as "humbug and nonsense" on the eve of President Bush's arrival.[13] After the president's visit, Musharraf charged that the insurgency was due to the internal weaknesses of Afghanistan, that Karzai was "totally oblivious of what is happening in his own country," and that there was a "conspiracy going on against Pakistan in [Karzai's] Ministry of Defense and his intelligence setup."[14] Musharraf claimed that India was feeding anti-Pakistan intelligence to Kabul. During President Karzai's visit to Islamabad, while Karzai and his intelligence chief presented (and leaked to the press) evidence of Taliban and al-Qaeda activities in

---

[12] Cooney, "Karzai Wants End to U.S.-Led Operations"; Jones, "Averting Failure in Afghanistan."
[13] "Martha Raddatz interview with President Musharraf," ABC News, February 27, 2006. Full transcript supplied by ABC News.
[14] "Pakistan President Blasts Afghan Leader," CNN.com, March 6, 2006.

Pakistan, the Pakistani intelligence agency made a presentation charging that intelligence agents in the Indian consulates in Jalalabad and Qandahar were funneling weapons and funds to opposition groups in Pakistan, in particular the insurgency in Baluchistan.

President Bush endorsed Musharraf's commitment to the war on terror, even as the latter admitted there had been some "slippage" in Pakistan's performance, perhaps alluding to the terrorist killing of a U.S. diplomat and four others in Karachi the day before Bush's arrival and the virtual occupation of the Waziristan Tribal Agencies by Taliban and foreign jihadists, who declared an Islamic state there. Pakistan launched a three-day offensive against these groups the day before Bush arrived, taking the town of Miram Shan and killing over one hundred guerrillas as ten thousand civilians fled the area. The magnitude of the engagement indicated the Taliban and foreign jihadists had a greater presence and more control of territory in Pakistan than in Afghanistan. American officials privately acknowledge that parts of the Pakistani state may not be fully on board. They argue that, given Musharraf's vulnerability (he has barely escaped assassination four times), Washington should stick to a policy of "public support and private pressure," so as to not destabilize the regime. This approach rests on the belief that stability in Pakistan depends solely on the military, a self-serving view promoted by the latter to their American counterparts for decades, and one that has survived the Bush administration's claim to move from a commitment to stability to a commitment to "freedom." President Bush did raise the issue of "democracy" during his visit, by which he apparently meant the holding of elections, but there is no indication that he discussed the fundamental issue of military dominance of the most important state institutions, including the judiciary.

Stabilizing this region requires a comprehensive policy toward the Afghanistan-Pakistan relationship, whose interaction with the India-Pakistan conflict has been the source of the region's troubles for nearly sixty years and now threatens global security. Although the most immediate issue is the bases and support networks for jihadi extremists in Pakistan, the use of these networks by the Pakistani military for several decades derives from that state's reliance on asymmetric warfare to compensate for its fundamental insecurity, which cannot be relieved solely by increasing pressure. Afghanistan and Pakistan will be unable to extricate themselves from this conflict without active engagement and assistance by the United States and other international actors to help them restructure their relationship in a more cooperative direction, including recognition of an international border and cooperative development of the tribal areas on either side. Any measure that lessens tension between India and Pakistan will also contribute to stability in the area, although how to bring that about is beyond the scope of this report.

Recommendations:

- The administration should insist on the Pakistani government's full cooperation in isolating and ending the neo-Taliban insurgency as part of a larger strategy that offers Pakistan benefits other than military equipment. In this component of the strategy, Washington must push for the Pakistani government to arrest Taliban leaders whose locations are provided by U.S. and Afghan intelligence agencies; take aggressive measures to close down the networks supporting suicide bombers that have been identified by those agencies; end public recruitment campaigns for the Taliban and pro-Taliban speeches at government institutions, including those by former leaders of Pakistan's Inter-Services Intelligence Directorate; close training camps (e.g., in Mansehra, Miramshah, and Shamshattu) for Taliban, including those for Kashmiri guerrillas where Taliban are trained; and cut off housing and pension benefits to retired military and government personnel engaged in supporting the Taliban. Until now the administration has conveyed mixed messages: when spokesmen praise Musharraf's cooperation against al-Qaeda, they have given the impression that ending sanctuary for the Taliban is a lower priority. Both public and private statements must place those engaged in violence in Afghanistan as equally threatening to U.S. interests and therefore of equal importance to the United States.

- The U.S. government must recognize that security in Afghanistan hinges on democratizing Pakistan. Military domination of the Pakistani state is the problem, not the solution. Elections will not democratize Pakistan as long as the military continues to control state institutions. The United States needs to signal at a high level that it wants to see the withdrawal of military control from Pakistan's civilian institutions and genuine freedom for political parties. It should support Pakistan's development by lifting restrictions on Pakistani textile imports into the United States, as Pakistani business has a strong economic interest in the stabilization of Afghanistan. This measure should not be held out as a reward for good behavior but should be enacted immediately to show commitment to cooperation with Pakistan on new terms.

- In response, Afghanistan will have to respect legitimate Pakistani concerns about the border and an Indian presence. Currently Afghanistan is following the historical pattern of turning to India to balance the threat from Pakistan, particularly in the context of the drawdown of U.S. forces and doubts about future U.S. commitment. The United States should strengthen its presence on the Afghan side of the border, and encourage India and Afghanistan not to engage in any provocative activity there. India has legitimate consular interests in Jalalabad and Qandahar involving Indian businesses and Afghan Sikhs and Hindus with family ties in India, but Afghanistan should encourage confidence-building measures with Pakistan in the area. Afghanistan also should refrain from relations with Pashtun leaders in Pakistan that give the impression that the government represents Pashtuns, which aggravates both relations with Pakistan and ethnic relations in Afghanistan.

- The United States should help Afghans realize that Islamabad will not respect a border that Kabul does not recognize. This is a very sensitive ethnic and political issue domestically, and it will be necessary to show that the border issue is not a zero-sum conflict and that recognizing the border need not isolate Pashtuns from each other, though they live in different states. Current efforts to promote development along the Durand line, bringing benefits to those on both sides, should be expanded, and both transit rights and access to Pakistani ports in Karachi and Gwadar should be guaranteed.

- Settling the border issue will require transforming the status of the tribal areas in Pakistan. Currently, these areas have lost their autonomy: they have experienced offensives by the Pakistani Army but have not enjoyed social and law enforcement services. The inhabitants of these areas must have the opportunity to participate in decisions about their future through genuine elections, which they have never had. Stabilizing the border also will require coordinated investments in the underdeveloped areas on both sides, although such coordination can be scaled up only as agreement on the political status of the border develops, and security threats no longer override other considerations.

- In order to launch a long-term program to stabilize and develop the Afghanistan-Pakistan border region, the United States and the UK should sponsor both official and second-track discussions involving all stakeholders in the border region. These discussions should ultimately aim to create a context in which Afghanistan can recognize an open border, the tribal territories of Pakistan can be integrated into and receive a full range of services from the Pakistani state, and the border area can become a region for cooperative development rather than insecurity, extremism, and antagonism.

OTHER REGIONAL DILEMMAS

Afghanistan's regional dilemmas go beyond Pakistan. Afghanistan's weakness has always posed a strategic dilemma for its rulers. Because the country has never produced enough wealth to pay the cost of governing or defending itself, Afghanistan has been stable only when its neighbors or imperial powers agreed to strengthen it as a buffer or nonaligned state to serve external security interests. The resulting lack of domestic legitimacy, however, has created opportunities for other foreign powers to interfere. Afghanistan's experience of interference after the Soviet withdrawal has intensified the country's mistrust of its neighbors and made many skeptical that nonalignment without effective deterrence of interference would suffice to guarantee the country's independence. Hence, Afghans tolerate international presence, including that of the U.S. military, as the needed deterrence to its neighbors' interference. Concerns that the United States might reduce its presence led President Karzai to seek long-term guarantees in the form of the Declaration of Strategic Partnership, which gave the United States the rights to military bases in Afghanistan and "freedom of action" for its forces.

Although Afghans largely accept the need for the U.S. presence, neither they nor the country's neighbors have accepted the overt nullification of the country's nonalignment that many saw in the Strategic Partnership. Soon after President Karzai announced his intention to seek such an agreement with the United States, demonstrations broke out around the country, in part against granting permanent bases to the United States. An underground leaflet ("Night Letter") circulating in Kabul during the rioting called Karzai a "U.S.A. servant" who put the interests of his "evil master" ahead of Afghanistan.[15]

Iran then drafted a proposed treaty with Afghanistan, including a provision that neither party would permit intelligence operations by third countries against the other. The United States opposed this treaty, which Afghanistan could not have enforced. When President Karzai wanted to visit Tehran for the inauguration of President Mahmoud Ahmadinejad on August 3, 2005, Iran told him he was not welcome if he would not sign the agreement. A call from U.S. Secretary of State Condoleezza Rice forced President Karzai to cancel a trip to Iran aimed at reaching economic agreements in January 2006. Afghanistan was caught between Tehran, which tried to use Afghanistan's need for transit to break out of its isolation over its nuclear program, and Washington, which deprived Kabul of the opportunity to exploit Tehran's discomfiture for its own benefit.

China and Russia issued veiled protests of Washington's actions in public and sharp rebukes in private. On July 5, 2005, the heads of state of the members of the Shanghai Cooperation Organization, which includes Russia, China, Kazakhstan, the Kyrgyz Republic, Tajikistan, and Uzbekistan, asked the United States to set a date for closing its military bases in Central Asia. These countries believe that the United States is exploiting their cooperation on counterterrorism to pursue long-term strategic objectives inimical to their interest. Subsequently, China and Russia conducted joint military operations on each other's territory for the first time, in part over these concerns.

Yet having good regional relations is extremely important to Afghanistan. Landlocked and arid, it can only economically develop through regional cooperation to manage its water resources, connect to the international market, and obtain energy. Because none of Afghanistan's neighbors welcomes a long-term U.S. military presence,

---

[15] John Lee Anderson, "The Man in the Palace," *New Yorker*, June 6, 2005.

they may resist such cooperation. Although the potential economic cooperation described in this report may help build confidence, regional cooperation will be limited in the absence of a U.S. understanding of Afghanistan's geopolitical and regional identity.

Recommendation:

- The United States and its Coalition partners, especially its principal NATO allies, should seek to promote a regional consensus on the geostrategic role of Afghanistan as a state not aligned against any neighbor. This requires developing understandings of how to insulate Afghanistan from conflicts in and over surrounding areas, including Iran, as was done for the first three decades of the Cold War and in the early part of the twentieth century, despite sharp political antagonisms in the region. Longer term stability in the region will be able to develop only as the Afghan state becomes stronger and able to articulate and implement relations with its neighbors. The United States should not undermine this eventual process by insisting that Afghanistan's foreign and security policy conform to U.S. strategic objectives. For instance, the United States has the means to confront the threat posed by Iran's nuclear program without forcing landlocked Afghanistan to forgo economic agreements with one of its most important partners for trade and transit, where over a million Afghans live.

STABILIZATION OPERATIONS

The Bonn Agreement defined the international stabilization mission in Afghanistan as helping Afghans to provide security until they were able to do so themselves. ISAF was confined to Kabul for nearly two years, and the Coalition did not initially define the domestic security of Afghanistan as part of its mission. Hence, militias and drug traffickers easily consolidated control of much of the country in 2002. Since late 2002, the Coalition has been devoting more resources to stabilization by means of the PRTs. Since ISAF expansion in 2003, NATO has been trying to field more troops and equipment, but it took NATO more than a year, from 2003 to 2004, to deploy a few transport helicopters.[16]

Some European NATO members are resisting unification of command with the Coalition that might lead to their troops' participation in counterinsurgency operations and lead them to turn over detainees to the U.S. government, in whose custody they risk treatment in violation of international humanitarian law.[17] They have now decided to turn prisoners over to the Afghan government on the condition that prisoners will neither be executed nor turned over to U.S. custody. Several troop contributors also have adopted national caveats for other reasons, even against proactive patrolling and measures to press for demobilization of militias. Success in Afghanistan, however, requires NATO contributors to find a way to carry out the mission while respecting international law, despite obstacles posed by the U.S. administration.

Recommendation:

- Troop contributors should adopt a common mission and rules of engagement, rather than insist on national caveats, even if this requires bilateral agreement with the Afghan government on treatment of prisoners or constructing separate detention facilities, to assure respect of Common Article 3 of the Geneva Conventions.

Provincial Reconstruction Teams

The PRT terms of reference now state that they will "assist the Islamic Republic of Afghanistan to extend its authority, to facilitate the development of a stable and secure environment in the identified area of operations, and enable SSR and reconstruction

---

[16] During his October 2005 trip to Kabul, NATO Secretary-General Jaap de Hoop Scheffer announced that NATO would increase its force in Afghanistan to as many as 15,000 soldiers and will take on counterinsurgency operations as it expands its mission into southern Afghanistan in the coming months. See Carlotta Gall, "NATO to Expand Force and Task In Afghanistan," *New York Times*, October 7, 2005.
[17] Eric Schmitt and David S. Cloud, "United States May Start Pulling Out of Afghanistan Next Spring," *New York Times*, September 14, 2005; James Travers, "Smart Move to Sidestep Afghanistan Prison Controversy," *The Hamilton Spectator* (Ontario, Canada), March 4, 2006.

18

efforts."[18] In response to Afghan concerns that PRTs were building projects that the government had no budget to operate, the Coalition now reviews projects to align them with Afghan government priorities. But the Coalition's development activities are still not integrated into the coordination procedures of the civilian aid donors, nor are military officers the best development partners for local administration.

Recommendation:

- PRTs should be reconfigured to support governance and development more effectively, by including more political officers and development specialists from NATO member countries, a possible role for the European Union. The development funds disbursed by PRTs should be subject to the same criteria for effectiveness as other assistance; those funds would be more effective if disbursements were accountable to provincial administration and elected councils, as through a trust fund.

Power-holder Impunity

Stabilization of the country will eventually require an end to the impunity of power holders. Despite several homicides by U.S. officials and contractors, and crimes by Afghan power holders including land grabbing, forced marriages, human trafficking, drug trafficking and other abuses, none of the guilty have received significant sanctions.

Recommendations:

- The United States must impose meaningful punishment on its personnel and contractors for homicides and torture of detainees.
- The Afghan government, with the support as needed of the Coalition and NATO, should begin a process to arrest powerful Afghan criminals (not just apolitical or pro-Taliban drug traffickers, as in the past year) and either punish or extradite them.

---

[18] Islamic Government of Afghanistan, "Terms of Reference for the Combined Force Command and ISAF PRTs in Afghanistan," January 27, 2005.

The Group of Eight (G8) adopted the current system of "lead donors" for SSR at the January 2002 Tokyo donor conference. The United States, with its focus on counterterrorism and reluctance to engage in "nation-building," took on building the Afghan National Army (ANA), while other donors took on other parts of the security sector. The fewer resources and lesser commitment by other actors in the lead-donor system have meant that development of the army is far ahead of that of the police, and both of these areas are more advanced than the justice system. A U.S.-led overhaul of the Ministry of the Interior and police began in late 2005. The Afghanistan Compact has brought this lead-donor system to a close, and SSR, like all other parts of the international effort, will be coordinated and monitored by a joint board cochaired by the Afghan government and the UN.

The irregular units initially absorbed into the Afghan Ministry of Defense (about 62,000 men) have been demobilized. The government and UN with Japanese funding have now launched programs for the disbandment of illegal armed groups (DIAG), of which there are an estimated 1,800, most of them quite small. Some leaders of these groups occupy seats in the National Assembly and posts in local administration. Strengthened vetting and enforcement could provide sanctions and incentives to disarm these groups, but DIAG will require much more Coalition and ISAF pressure on commanders and political leaders. As former Minister of the Interior Ali Jalali has observed:

> The United States has long hesitated to support the removal of defiant warlords....While the PRTs are mandated to help extend the authority of the central government and facilitate stability, in certain cases they have discouraged government action against spoilers because of concerns about their own security....However, failure to hold [militia leaders] accountable...continues to undermine the establishment of the rule of law.[19]

---

[19] Ali A. Jalali, "The Future of Afghanistan," *Parameters* (Spring 2006), p. 6.

Using pressure to hold such leaders accountable and disarm them does not mean warfare but rather local negotiations backed up with pressure and threats when needed. Leaders and members of armed groups were supposed to be banned from running for parliament or the provincial councils, and the Coalition offered to help cope with resistance from potential candidates during the vetting process, indicating the military's estimate that such actions would not lead to warfare.

Recommendation:

- The Coalition and ISAF should increase pressure, in cooperation with the Afghan government, on commanders and political leaders to disarm and demobilize illegal armed groups. NATO and the U.S. Department of Defense should issue clear guidance authorizing PRTs to engage in this process robustly. What is needed is a capacity for local coercive diplomacy. Coalition forces have occasionally taken such actions, by briefly firing on a group that refused to disarm or buzzing the house of a leading warlord with fighter aircraft. These incidents always ended peacefully soon after, as these groups are opportunistic rather than ideological in motivation.

The United States, with aid from France and the United Kingdom, has been training a new national army, which has now reached about 26,000 troops. The ANA was designed by the Department of Defense, and it deploys troops with embedded U.S. trainers. The U.S. model of an army, however, has a high price tag. According to the World Bank, the ANA cost 13 percent of gross domestic product (GDP) in fiscal year 2004–2005, and total security sector spending topped 17 percent.[20] Currently, the ANA depends on U.S. trainers for air support, logistics, and medical evacuation. Transferring the ownership of these functions to the ANA will cost even more.

The Coalition has slowed ANA growth. Defense Secretary Donald Rumsfeld informed the Afghan government that the United States will expect it to pay the military's salaries from its budget in 2006–2007. According to Afghan sources, he also

---

[20] World Bank, *Afghanistan: Managing Public Finances for Development, Main Report*, vol. 1 (Washington, DC: World Bank, November 27, 2005), p. 24.

told Kabul that the ceiling for the ANA would be 45,000 men, compared to the 70,000 that the Afghan Ministry of Defense thinks it needs.

Although the belated concern for fiscal sustainability is welcome, this unilateral decision has placed the Afghans in a difficult position. The United States, not Afghanistan, determined the salary levels of the ANA, and now the United States is insisting that this impoverished, insecure country, just embarking on a major development strategy, take on this fiscal burden. Secretary Rumsfeld has reportedly assured the Afghans that the United States will ensure Afghanistan's external security, but the failure of the United States to neutralize the Taliban and al-Qaeda sanctuaries in Pakistan has made the Afghans skeptical of such guarantees.

Because Afghanistan cannot have a foreign-supported army for long, some adjustment of the quantity or quality of the force is inevitable. Besides simply making the ANA smaller, the Afghan government could move away from the U.S.-inspired structure toward a more cost-effective, if less professional, army, such as one based on conscription and compensation in kind (housing and other facilities) rather than cash. Similar adjustments must be made for the Afghan National Police (ANP). Current plans to raise police salaries to a level comparable to that of the ANA will further inflate the budget beyond the country's means. Because of the insufficiency of both international and national security forces, the Afghan government continues to raise informal militias, mostly in Pashtun areas, where the Taliban are active. This has created some anxiety among non-Pashtuns, who have seen their much larger militias disbanded. The need for regional and ethnic equity must be taken into account in the structure of the security forces.

Recommendations:

- The Afghan government and its partners in SSR should reexamine the structure and mission of the army and police as the Afghan security sector must be fiscally sustainable. To enable the ANA to become more self-sufficient, the force may need to be smaller than initially planned and more cost-effective. This may require a change from the U.S.-inspired model of a highly paid, all-volunteer army.

- The central police force also must be relatively small to be effective and affordable. Rather than trying to deploy a centralized security force throughout the country, the government should police the cities, main roads, border points, and national installations, while organizing, disciplining, and lightly subsidizing locally based forces in much of the country.

- Coalition forces should reduce intrusive foreign presence in the security forces. The Coalition must begin planning a reduction of the pervasive role the United States plays in the ANA. Embedded advisers planned for the ANP should not patrol.

GOVERNANCE, RULE OF LAW, AND HUMAN RIGHTS

The compact provides benchmarks for strengthening democratic institutions, in particular the National Assembly and other elected bodies, and for building the capacity and accountability of the administration. It emphasizes reforming the judiciary and strengthening the rule of law, including the protection of human rights. It provides for implementation of a transitional justice action plan to confront the past abuses.

JUDICIAL REFORM

Police cannot provide security without courts. The judiciary is the sole part of the state still dominated by the ulama, the learned clergy, who play a central role in determining—and undermining—the legitimacy of governments. Hence, judicial reform involves sensitive issues. By now, however, the lack of judicial reform has become a bottleneck for security, governance, and economic development.

The judiciary has been headed by Chief Justice Fazl Hadi Shinwari, who is also head of the official Council of Ulama. Shinwari is widely reported to be corrupt, his legal scholarship appears deficient, and he has offended many with his conservative views against gender equality. Nonetheless, President Karzai has found him useful in maintaining the consent of religious leaders to the system of government and the international presence. Shinwari has also used his Islamic credentials to negotiate with Taliban who wish to surrender to the government.

As the Afghan Supreme Court is the administrative as well as judicial head of the court system, President Karzai's appointment of a new supreme court, as required by the constitution, is critical to reform. If the new judicial appointments simply appease the most conservative elements, reform will stall again. But if the new supreme court includes more progressive Islamic scholars, it can transform many of the ulama into allies in the process.

Afghans also have shown that they want and need some reckoning with their immense suffering over the past several decades. At the same time, many of those now in positions of power or influence are widely held to be responsible for past crimes. The Afghan government has adopted the Action Plan on Transitional Justice and the compact requires it to implement this plan by 2008. The groups that formed the Northern Alliance fear that this process will be used against them, as they are political competitors with the president, and will spare both the communists, who now claim to support democracy, and the Taliban, who are being wooed to put down their arms. The implementation of this program should remove any such suspicion.

Recommendations:

- President Karzai should replace Shinwari as chief justice and form a court composed of judges of top legal, scholarly, and personal credentials, trained in Islamic, civil, and constitutional law, including Shi'a and women.
- Donors should support efforts to engage rather than confront or appease the ulama by reviving engagement of Afghan Islamic scholars with the main centers of learning in the Islamic world, as existed decades ago.
- Donor countries and the UN should support implementation of the Action Plan on Transitional Justice without politicizing it. Assure that this process examines abuses by communists, mujahidin, other militias, Taliban, and foreign forces (Soviet, Pakistani, al-Qaeda, American) impartially with a view to establishing truth, reconciliation, and justice.

GOVERNMENT INSTITUTIONS

The convening of the National Assembly on December 19, 2005, following the September 18, 2005, elections to the lower house and provincial councils, effectively completed the Bonn process, which aimed at reestablishing permanent institutions of government. The election of representatives, however, is a means to the accountable provision of public services by the state. If the state is incapable of providing those public services, elections can lead to kleptocracy rather than democracy, and many Afghans fear that this process is already under way.

Resources

Afghanistan has one of the weakest governments in the world. The International Monetary Fund (IMF) estimates that the government revenue will total 5.4 percent of nondrug GDP in 2005–2006, less than any country with data. Furthermore, the administration has difficulty disbursing the funds it has: the ten poorest provinces receive the smallest budgetary allocations, leading to nonexistent government presence and rampant security problems.[21]

Attempts to raise domestic revenue are stymied by the lack of control over the country's borders, the small portion of the economy in the formal legal sector, and the weakness and corruption of the administration, particularly in tax collection. Currently, would-be tax payers are discouraged by collectors, who suggest they pay bribes instead.

The Afghanistan Compact requires the government to raise domestic revenue to over 8 percent of GDP by fiscal year 2011 and to be able to cover 58 percent of the recurrent budget with its own resources, compared to 28 percent in fiscal year 2005. Nonetheless, escalating costs of security and civil service reform will make these targets difficult to achieve.

Recommendations:
- The Coalition and Afghan government should support continuing fiscal reform, including ISAF and Coalition military deployments in support of control of borders (for revenue collection) and state banks (for expenditure). The government should rationalize the procedures for business taxation, abolish nuisance taxes, and find other ways to tax the expenditures of the international

---

[21] Ashraf Ghani, Clare Lockhart, Baqer Massoud, and Nargis Nehan, "Public Finance in Afghanistan: The Budget as the Instrument of State-Building and Policymaking," in James Boyce, ed., *Peace and the Public Purse: Building State Capacity after Violent Conflict* (New York: Center on International Cooperation, forthcoming).

presence, as it has done through rent taxes. For instance, the government could tax non-work-related imports.

- Aid programs should assist the ministry of finance in establishing electronic tax payment, revenue tracking, and expenditure systems, compatible with the treasury system already in place. Developing and funding of programs, including those sponsored by PRTs, through the Afghan budgetary process, rather than through independent donor mechanisms, is essential to developing a fiscally sustainable state.

Administration and Service Provision

The government has started reforms at the national level, but many ministries are still nonfunctional or corrupt. The provincial and district administrations, the face of government for most Afghans, are largely controlled by illicit or violent power holders.

In Afghanistan's centralized unitary state, the president appoints all ministers, deputy ministers, governors, and provincial security chiefs. The character of these appointees is one of the important political issues in the country. The Afghanistan Compact requires the government to establish formal vetting procedures by an independent board for senior appointments. This board would vet potential appointees for qualifications and involvement with drug trafficking, corruption, armed groups, or past human rights violations.

Recommendation:

- In addition to confidential vetting, the Afghan appointments board should introduce more transparency into the appointments process. Candidates should be required to make public their assets, as is required for the most senior figures by article 154 of the constitution, and extend this requirement to their families. Appointments of deputy ministers, governors, district officers, and provincial and district police chiefs should also be announced for public comment thirty days before taking effect.

Corruption

Afghanistan's weak administration has few if any effective controls over corruption, which has undermined support for the government. Some systems have been instituted to prevent the most important types of corruption, notably a system requiring transparent public bidding for procurement. Increasingly, however, ministries are sidestepping this procedure and signing single-source contracts, many of which are then approved by the president in the interest of not delaying important projects. The compact obliges the government to fight corruption without saying how.

Recommendation:

- The Afghan president should tell his cabinet that he will no longer sign single-source contracts without exceptional circumstances and that all ministers found proffering such contracts will be sacked. International donors should invest in building the capacity of the Afghan government to draft proposals and process contracts so that transparent procedures do not lead to intolerable delays.

Self-governance

At the local level, Afghans' self-governance institutions have enabled people to survive even when the central government collapsed. This capacity for self-government could bode well for the country's future, except that these institutions function largely outside the constitutional system. The framers of the country's 2004 constitution followed historical precedent in mandating a highly centralized administrative system. Although elected provincial councils have been formed, these have only advisory and watchdog roles. The budgets of the village-level Community Development Councils (CDCs) created by the National Solidarity Program (NSP) are limited to block grants for specific projects approved by the ministry of rural rehabilitation and development.

Even within a unitary system, however, the delivery of services and accountability for public expenditure can be devolved to lower levels of government, creating potential for integrating local governance into the state. Unintentionally, the PRTs have for the first time in the history of Afghanistan introduced provincial development budgets. Currently, these are controlled by foreign officials of the PRTs, who disburse the funds with varying degrees of consultation with local authorities and society. From the bottom up, in a number of cases village CDCs have banded together to formulate district-level or larger projects for funding by the NSP. These show the potential for devolution.

Recommendation:

- The Afghan government should introduce measure to devolve service provision in Afghanistan's unitary state. As the provincial councils elected in September 2005 start to work, both they and the provincial administration should gradually gain greater oversight over provincial expenditures, including those by PRTs. The government and donors also should do more to encourage grassroots development cooperation by empowering provincial councils and administration to coordinate local development activities.

Integration of Religious Institutions

Afghanistan is an Islamic Republic, and Islamic institutions form part of the governance structure. The ulama are organized through the judiciary, the Council of Ulama, and the Ministry of Irshad (Instruction), Hajj (Pilgrimage), and Awqaf (Islamic foundations), which pays the salaries of official mullahs. Many "unofficial" mullahs are paid directly by the faithful through what are considered to be Islamic taxes, rather than voluntary donations. Mosques are centers not only for prayer and instruction, but for community self-governance and service provision. The ministry and the ulama council can distribute weekly talking points for the Friday sermon to virtually every village.

This sermon, or khutba, is the main means through which the ulama communicate their views to the people. Khutbas now often highlight moral corruption, the increasing gap between rich and poor, and misdeeds by the Coalition. These sermons reflect debate among the ulama over whether the new government is Islamic and whether the presence of non-Muslim forces in Afghanistan is legitimate. The government, short of budgetary resources, has been removing mullahs from the payroll. Many laid-off mullahs continue to be paid, by either local power holders (often involved in the drug trade) or international Islamic sources.

The government and donors should proactively prevent the growth of religiously oriented opposition. Mosque management and the Council of Ulama need reform. Dropping mullahs from the payroll simply for lack of resources, or building mosques to show that the United States is not anti-Islamic (as some PRTs have done) without a strategy or policy is dangerous. The social capital that village mosques embody should be mobilized on behalf of the reconstruction of the country and the strengthening of its constitutional institutions.

Recommendation:

- The Afghan government should bring the mosque-based traditional village administration and dispute settlement procedures gradually into the ambit of state institutions. Donors should support this sensitive aspect of building an Islamic state.

ECONOMIC AND SOCIAL DEVELOPMENT

Basic indicators of human welfare place Afghans among a handful of the world's most hungry, destitute, illiterate, and short-lived people. The country ranks approximately 173 out of 178 countries in the basic index of human development, effectively putting it in a tie for last place with a few African countries.[22] Afghan women face the highest rates of illiteracy and the lowest standards of health in the world. Afghanistan has the youngest population in the world (an estimated 57 percent under eighteen years old) with few employment prospects in the offing.[23]

The livelihoods of the people of this impoverished, devastated country are more dependent on illegal narcotics than any other country in the world. According to estimates by the UN and IMF, the total export value of opiates produced in Afghanistan in 2005–2006 equaled about 38 percent of nondrug GDP, down from 47 percent the previous year due to growth of the nondrug economy. Much of the trafficking profits do not enter the Afghan economy, but even if only one-third of trafficking income stayed in the country, the direct contribution to the domestic economy would amount to 15 percent of the total, with more attributable to the multiplier effect of drug-financed spending. The UN estimates that in recent years nearly 80 percent of the income from narcotics went not to farmers but to traffickers and heroin processors, some of whose profits corrupt the government and support armed groups.[24] The distribution of the proceeds of narcotics trafficking, not elections, largely determines who wields power in much of Afghanistan.

---

[22] Along with Somalia, Afghanistan is one of two countries in the world unable to produce accurate enough data to be ranked in UN Development Programme's annual Human Development Report. Using available data, however, Afghanistan's *National Human Development Report 2004* estimated that Afghanistan would have ranked 173 out of 178, barely ahead of the African states of Chad, Mali, Burkina Faso, Sierra Leone, and Niger. UNDP, *Afghanistan: National Human Development Report 2004*, http://hdr.undp.org/docs/ reports/national/AFG_Afghanistan/afghanistan_2004_en.pdf.

[23] For population statistics on Afghanistan see Afghanistan's Millennium Development Goal report: http://www.ands.gov.af/src/src/MDGs_Reps/MDGR%202005.pdf.

[24] UN Office on Drugs and Crime and Government of Afghanistan Counter Narcotics Directorate, *Afghanistan: Opium Survey 2005*, p. 9, http://www.unodc.org/pdf/afg/afg_survey_2005_exsum.pdf.

Against this somber background, Afghanistan has experienced an economic recovery. The IMF estimates that real, nondrug GDP has averaged annual growth of nearly 17 percent from 2001–2002 through 2005–2006. The government has sought to set its development agenda, rather than ceding it to aid organizations. At the London conference it presented its I-ANDS, which international financial institutions hailed as one of the best they have received from any developing country.

Nevertheless, the postwar economic boom is coming to an end. The IMF warns that the sources of the rebound "will be insufficient over the long term to sustain growth and alleviate poverty." Additionally, counternarcotics policies, if implemented wrongly, risk reversing the economic recovery that has helped stabilize the country. An as yet unpublished macroeconomic simulation by an international financial institution demonstrates that different types of counternarcotics policies have different macroeconomic impacts and that a strategy including eradication at early stages can lead to a contraction of total GDP by nearly 6 percent. A change from recent rapid GDP growth of nearly 20 percent per year to a significant contraction is likely to provoke instability and violence. The provision of "alternative livelihoods" to farmers alone would not fully compensate for the effect of such an economic contraction on poverty, nutrition, health, employment, investment, the balance of payments, the exchange rate, and the price level. Donor countries are threatening to limit their aid if narcotics production is not curbed quickly, regardless of its economic effects. The U.S. Congress "fenced" part of this year's aid disbursement, pending certification by President Bush that Afghanistan was cooperating with U.S. counternarcotics policies.

Recommendations:

- The main counternarcotics goal should be reducing the absolute and relative economic size of the opium economy while maintaining positive growth that favors the poor in the overall economy.[25]

---

[25] The "poor" in Afghanistan are defined as either: (1) those without enough food to meet basic caloric needs consistently (about 40 percent of the rural population); or (2) those living on less than one U.S. dollar

- Counternarcotics development strategies must be comprehensive, not make-work programs. "Alternative livelihoods" need to include comprehensive rural development, including electric power, water, roads, credit, debt relief, agricultural extension, and non-farm employment, particularly in rural industries. Counternarcotics policy must also address the macroeconomic measures needed to minimize the negative effect of this sector's contraction on the whole economy. Such policies need over a decade to become fully effective.

This goal focuses on reducing the harm to the stability of Afghanistan, rather than following the illusory course of trying to solve the problem of drug consumption—which developed countries have not been able to solve with all the resources available to them —in the world's weakest state. Hence, the I-ANDS and the Afghan government's new Drugs Control Policy propose a "pro-poor" counternarcotics policy that focuses initially on interdiction, law enforcement, institution building, and building licit livelihoods, while investing in infrastructure, protection of rights, and an enabling framework for private sector growth that will make it possible to raise welfare while phasing out dependence on criminal activity. Crop eradication, which the U.S. Congress in particular views as critical, despite massive evidence to the contrary, raises the farm price of opium, creates incentives for production in remote high-cost areas, and raises the value of traffickers' inventories. Eradication in Afghanistan has led to abuses such as the sale of daughters by opium farmers to pay debts owed to traffickers.[26]

Recommendations:

- To assure that counternarcotics and economic development both contribute to stabilizing Afghanistan, the United States and other donors must support the integrated approach of the I-ANDS.

- The U.S. government should support the Afghan government's National Drugs Control Policy. Congress should not undermine these efforts by insisting on U.S. contracting, earmarking for particular projects or causes, such as aerial eradication

---

per day (for which data are not yet available). Pro-poor growth is important because the few rich will otherwise monopolize most of the benefits of investment.

[26] Farah Stockman, "Afghan Women Pay the Price for War on Drugs," *Boston Globe*, September 29, 2005.

(which the Afghan government opposes), or conditioning support on quick results.

- The preferred method for supporting counternarcotics is by contributing to the Counternarcotics Trust Fund managed by the United Nations Development Programme (UNDP). NATO and the Coalition should support Afghan-led interdiction operations, especially those directed against heroin processing and narcotics inventories, and adopt a common mission and rules of engagement on counternarcotics. In much of the country, narcotics interdiction of high-level trafficking has proceeded without generating massive resistance. An exception is Hilmand, where the British PRT is working with the governor to devise a strategy to address the strong links in that area between traffickers and the Taliban and other armed groups. Thus far, however, crop eradication has generated more violent resistance than interdiction. The Afghan drug market has so far not generated violent cartels; rather, it has remained more fragmented and competitive.

FINANCING PRO-POOR GROWTH

All efforts to stabilize Afghanistan will fail if the licit economy does not expand fast enough to provide enough employment, income, and investment to more than balance the loss of income from opiates and provide a fiscal basis for expanding public services. In 2004, the Afghan government estimated it would cost $27.6 billion to achieve stabilization goals over seven years with disbursements over twelve years starting in 2004–2005; the I-ANDS tentatively revised this estimate upward. Initially, the resources devoted to Afghanistan hardly corresponded to the Marshall Plan to which President Bush compared the reconstruction of Afghanistan in April 2002.[27] Figure 2 compares troop presence and per capita aid to Afghanistan during the first two years of the transitional period with other stabilization operations. These figures do not include the

---

[27] President George W. Bush, "Remarks on war effort delivered to the George C. Marshall ROTC Award Seminar on National Security at Cameron Hall," Virginia Military Institute, Lexington, Virginia, April 17, 2002, available at http://www.whitehouse.gov/news/releases/2002/04/20020417-1.html.

military operations of the Coalition or ISAF, both of which cost far more than the assistance budget. During 2002–2003, Afghanistan was far below all Balkan operations, East Timor, and Iraq, and even below Namibia and Haiti. After this slow start, especially by the United States, funding for reconstruction is increasing toward the rate needed to meet the target of $27.6 billion. The cost of delivery of assistance, however, has been higher than expected, so that the money expended has produced less on the ground than planned, and much of the increase in aid has gone to the security sector, which has cost far more than projected.

Figure 2: Security and Economic Assistance in Peace/Nation/State Building Operations*

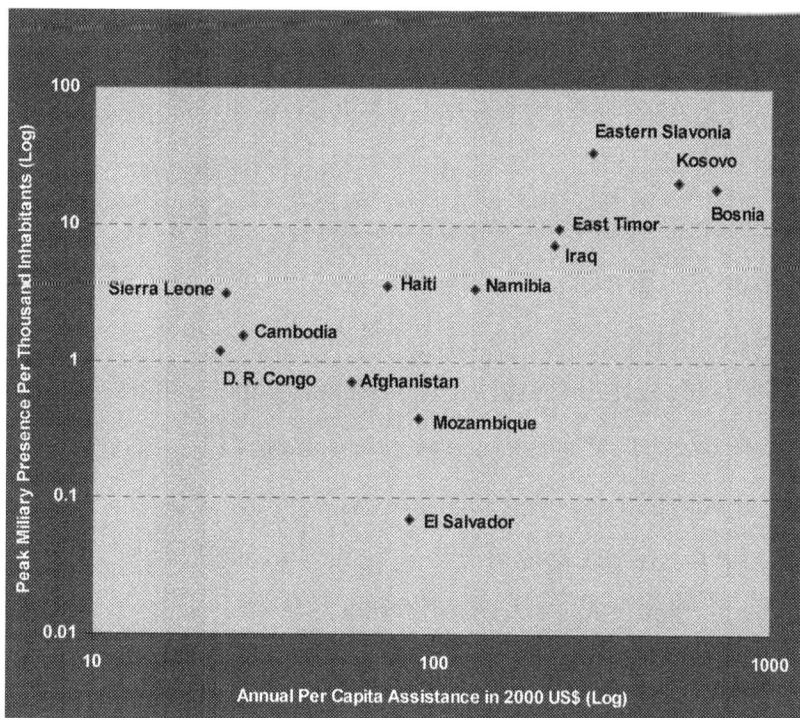

* Shows peak security presence and average yearly per capita economic assistance for the first two years of each operation, including Afghanistan in 2002–2003.

Source: Barnett R. Rubin, *The Road to Ruin: Afghanistan's Drug Economy*, Center for American Progress and Center on International Cooperation, September 2004; data from James Dobbins et al., *The UN's Role in Nation-Building: From the Congo To Iraq* (Santa Monica: RAND Corporation, 2005).

As shown in figure 3, U.S. pledges of assistance rose dramatically in 2004–2005, as Presidential Special Envoy and Ambassador Zalmay Khalilzad presided over a program called "Accelerate Success," intended to build support for President Karzai during his election campaign. Figure 3 also shows, however, that the United States was not able to match disbursements to its pledges and commitments.[28] Instead, the pressure for politically motivated quick results led to waste and failure to deliver on Afghans' expectations.[29] Other donors have experienced similar problems, but they are particularly severe for the United States.[30]

The Afghanistan Compact includes an annex on aid effectiveness. The Afghan government commits itself to transparency and accountability, to raising more domestic resources, and to improving its capacity to manage expenditure and implement programs. In return, the donors agree to allocate their assistance according to ANDS priorities; provide "multiyear funding commitments or indications of multiyear support"; increase untied aid channeled through the government budget; build Afghan capacity; and report on aid in a way that enables the Afghan government to integrate aid into its national budget and reports on its use to the National Assembly.[31]

More than 75 percent of all aid to Afghanistan funds projects directly implemented or contracted by donors. This mode of delivery, although initially inevitable, is ultimately self-defeating. If prolonged, it undermines, not builds, the state. Enabling the state to provide services directly promotes legitimacy and responsibility; integrating aid projects into the budgetary process promotes sustainability. A government that cannot report to its parliament about public expenditure can hardly be called democratic, no matter how many elections it holds.

---

[28] A pledge is a promise of an amount; a commitment is a signed contract for a specific use of funds. Commitments lead to disbursements, which are deposits in to the accounts of trust funds or implementing agencies. Disbursed funds are turned into expenditures as projects are implemented, which can take years in some cases. Donors report on disbursement, which constitutes expenditure by the donor government, but not on final expenditure on development, which is of greatest interest to the aid recipient.

[29] See Carlotta Gall and Somini Sengupta, "Afghan Electorate's Message: The Provinces Need Public Works and Restoration of Order," *New York Times*, September 20, 2005.

[30] Data from the Ministry of Finance for aid through the end of calendar year 2005 show that the United States had disbursed 36 percent of commitments for that year, compared to 58 percent for other donors.

[31] The World Bank–administered Afghanistan Reconstruction Trust Fund supports the government's recurrent and development expenditures. Trust funds managed by the UNDP provide support for SSR and counternarcotics.

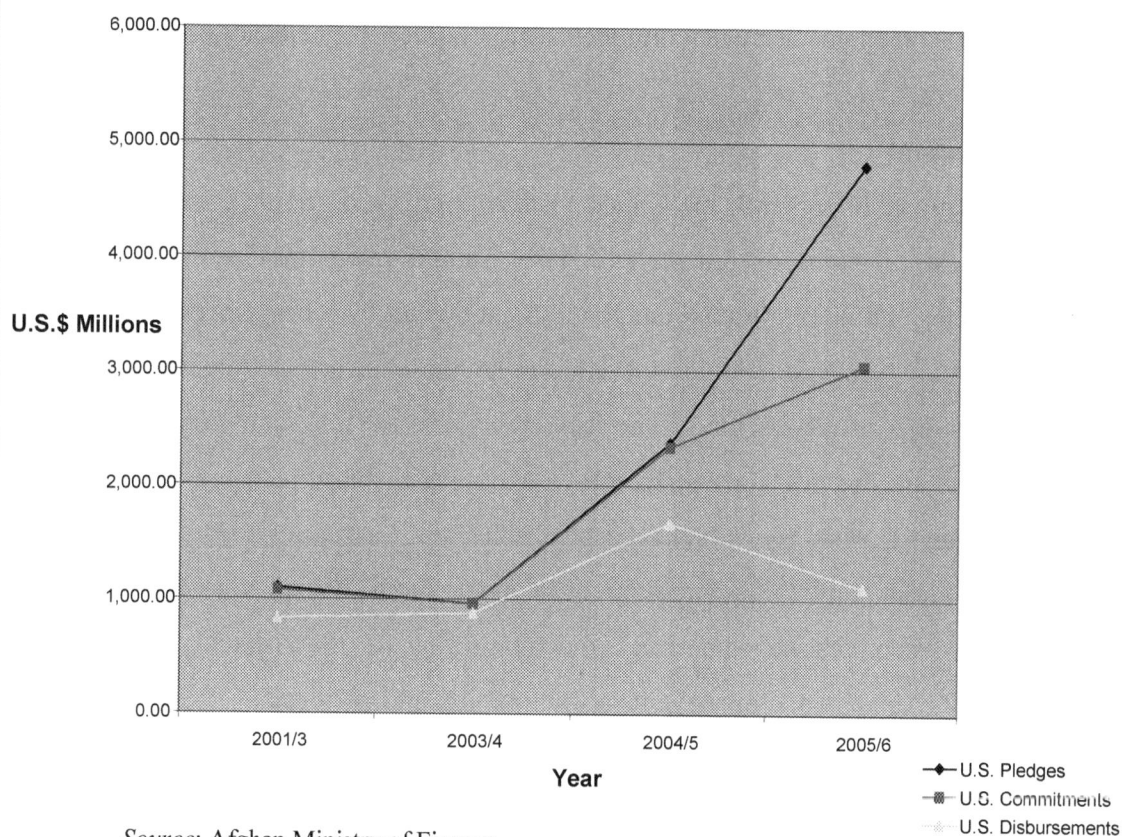

Figure 3: Assistance to Afghanistan

Source: Afghan Ministry of Finance.

Three of the largest donors, however—the United States, Japan, and Germany—insisted on weakening these provisions. U.S. officials claim that the U.S. government's fiduciary responsibility to taxpayers makes it difficult to channel money through the Afghan government's budget. Like other donors, the United States cites the prevalence of corruption and lack of capacity in Afghanistan, which are valid concerns, though they do not prevent the UK from channeling aid through the budget. The argument of fiduciary responsibility, however, collapses under the weight of evidence of what the U.S. government actually does with much of taxpayers' money in Afghanistan. It disburses it to U.S.-based contractors who spend a significant (and unreported) part of the funds setting up office. In one case, their services were of such poor quality that the Afghan ministry they were supposed to help expelled them. Security regulations sometimes prevent U.S. contractors from implementing projects in the field and impose significant

37

additional costs. Both the fiduciary responsibility to the U.S. taxpayer and the policy goals of the U.S. government would often be accomplished better by direct budgetary support to the Afghan government, combined with programs for capacity building.

Recommendation:

- International donors, and the United States in particular, should give aid in accord with the priorities of the ANDS. They should overcome legal and political obstacles to funding through the government budget by setting specific criteria for doing so. Congress should not undermine these efforts by insisting on U.S. contracting or earmarking. The best mechanisms for such direct budgetary support are the Afghanistan Reconstruction Trust Fund managed by the World Bank and the two funds managed by UNDP, the Law and Order Trust Fund for Afghanistan, and the Counternarcotics Trust Fund. These trust funds provide strong incentives, benchmarking, and monitoring for the Afghan government to build its capacity and improve its accountability and performance.

REGIONAL DIMENSIONS OF RECONSTRUCTION

Afghanistan's development requires cooperation of this landlocked country with its neighbors, especially Pakistan and Iran, which provide outlets to the sea.[32] Without confidence in regional security arrangements, neighboring countries may resist the economic and infrastructural integration that is indispensable for Afghanistan's future.

Recommendations:

- The United States and other donors should support regional economic cooperation, including in infrastructure, trade and transit, water use, energy, migration and manpower, and development of border regions, by establishing dedicated funding frameworks for regional economic cooperation in this region.

---

[32] See Barnett R. Rubin with Andrea Armstrong, "Regional Issues in the Reconstruction of Afghanistan," *World Policy Journal*, Vol. 20, No. 1 (Spring 2003), pp. 37–48, and S. Frederick Starr, "A Partnership for Central Asia," *Foreign Affairs* (July/August 2005).

This will require both national budget lines for regional cooperation and funding mechanisms, such as a trust fund for development of regional cooperation in support of the development and stabilization of Afghanistan.

- The United States and its allies, perhaps through NATO, should initiate high-level discussions to insulate Afghan economic development from conflict with Iran or concerns over the Coalition military presence.

CONCLUSION

The sketch of Afghanistan's problems in this report is meant to be realistic; these are the challenges facing Afghanistan. We already know that the cost of failing is virtually incalculable. The Afghanistan Compact provides many elements of a plan for sustainable security, governance, and development. This report has tried to supplement that by suggesting additional measures for implementation. If the international community is unable or unwilling to meet the cost of success, or if Afghan authorities are unable or unwilling to make the decisions needed to use assistance effectively, they must answer the question: What risks are they willing to accept? Afghans are determined not to revert to a past they abhor; will their leaders and international actors enable them to succeed?

ABOUT THE AUTHOR

Barnett R. Rubin is director of studies and senior fellow at the Center on International Cooperation at New York University. From November to December 2001, he served as adviser to the UN special representative of the secretary-general for Afghanistan, Lakhdar Brahimi, during the negotiations that produced the Bonn Agreement. From 1994 to 2000, he was director of the Center for Preventive Action and director of peace and conflict studies at the Council on Foreign Relations in New York.

Previously, Dr. Rubin was associate professor of political science and director of the Center for the Study of Central Asia at Columbia University, Jennings Randolph peace fellow at the United States Institute of Peace, and assistant professor of political science at Yale University. He is considered one of the world's foremost experts on Afghanistan, conflict prevention, and peacebuilding, and is the author of several books, including *Blood on the Doorstep: The Politics of Preventing Violent Conflict* (2002); *Calming the Ferghana Valley: Development and Dialogue in the Heart of Central Asia* (1999); and *The Search for Peace in Afghanistan: From Buffer State to Failed State* (1995).

MISSION STATEMENT OF THE CENTER FOR PREVENTIVE ACTION

The Center for Preventive Action seeks to help prevent, defuse, or resolve deadly conflicts around the world and to expand the body of knowledge on conflict prevention. It does so by creating a forum in which representatives of governments, international organizations, nongovernmental organizations, corporations, and civil society can gather to develop operational and timely strategies for promoting peace in specific conflict situations. The center focuses on conflicts in countries or regions that affect U.S. interests, but may be otherwise overlooked; where prevention appears possible; and when the resources of the Council on Foreign Relations can make a difference. The center does this by:

- *Convening Independent Preventive Action Commissions* composed of Council members, staff, and other experts. The commissions devise a practical, actionable conflict-prevention strategy tailored to the facts of the particular situation.

- *Issuing Council Special Reports* to evaluate and respond rapidly to developing conflict situations and formulate timely, concrete policy recommendations that the U.S. government, international community, and local actors can use to limit the potential for deadly violence.

- *Engaging the U.S. government and news media* in conflict prevention efforts. The center's staff and commission members meet with administration officials and members of Congress to brief them on CPA's findings and recommendations; facilitate contacts between U.S. officials and key local and external actors; and raise awareness among journalists of potential flashpoints around the globe.

- *Building networks with international organizations and institutions* to complement and leverage the Council's established influence in the U.S. policy arena and increase the impact of CPA's recommendations.

- *Providing a source of expertise on conflict prevention* to include research, case studies, and lessons learned from past conflicts that policymakers and private citizens can use to prevent or mitigate future deadly conflicts.

CENTER FOR PREVENTIVE ACTION ADVISORY COMMITTEE

John W. Vessey Jr., USA
GENERAL, USA (RET.);
CHAIR, CPA ADVISORY
COMMITTEE

Morton I. Abramowitz
THE CENTURY FOUNDATION

Patrick M. Byrne
OVERSTOCK.COM

Antonia Handler Chayes
TUFTS UNIVERSITY

Leslie H. Gelb
COUNCIL ON FOREIGN RELATIONS

Joachim Gfoeller Jr.
G.M.G. CAPITAL PARTNERS, L.P.

Richard N. Haass
COUNCIL ON FOREIGN RELATIONS

David A. Hamburg
CORNELL UNIVERSITY MEDICAL
COLLEGE

John G. Heimann
FINANCIAL STABILITY INSTITUTE

George A. Joulwan
GENERAL, USA (RET.);
ONE TEAM, INC.

Jane Holl Lute
UNITED NATIONS

Vincent A. Mai
AEA INVESTORS INC.

Margaret Farris Mudd
FINANCIAL SERVICES
VOLUNTEER CORPS

Kenneth Roth
HUMAN RIGHTS WATCH

Barnett R. Rubin
NEW YORK UNIVERSITY

Julia Vadala Taft

Robert G. Wilmers
MANUFACTURERS & TRADERS
TRUST CO.

OTHER COUNCIL SPECIAL REPORTS
SPONSORED BY THE COUNCIL ON FOREIGN RELATIONS

Preventing Catastrophic Nuclear Terrorism
Charles D. Ferguson; CSR No. 11, March 2006

Getting Serious About the Twin Deficits
Menzie D. Chinn; CSR No. 10, September 2005

Both Sides of the Aisle: A Call for Bipartisan Foreign Policy
Nancy E. Roman; CSR No. 9, September 2005

Forgotten Intervention? What the United States Needs to Do in the Western Balkans
Amelia Branczik and William L. Nash; CSR No. 8, June 2005

A New Beginning: Strategies for a More Fruitful Dialogue with the Muslim World
Craig Charney and Nicole Yakatan; CSR No. 7, May 2005

Power-Sharing in Iraq
David L. Phillips; CSR No. 6, April 2005

Giving Meaning to "Never Again": Seeking an Effective Response to the Crisis in Darfur and Beyond
Cheryl O. Igiri and Princeton N. Lyman; CSR No. 5, September 2004

Freedom, Prosperity, and Security: The G8 Partnership with Africa: Sea Island 2004 and Beyond
J. Brian Atwood, Robert S. Browne, and Princeton N. Lyman; CSR No. 4, May 2004

Addressing the HIV/AIDS Pandemic: A U.S. Global AIDS Strategy for the Long Term
Daniel M. Fox and Princeton N. Lyman; CSR No. 3, May 2004
Cosponsored with the Milbank Memorial Fund

Challenges for a Post-Election Philippines
Catharin E. Dalpino; CSR No. 2, May 2004

Stability, Security, and Sovereignty in the Republic of Georgia
David L. Phillips; CSR No. 1, January 2004

To purchase a hard copy, please contact the Brookings Institution Press: 800-537-5487
Note: All these reports are available on the Council's website at www.cfr.org, along with a complete list of the Council publications since 1998. For more information, contact publications@cfr.org.